PLANT MILK
POWER

DELICIOUS, NUTRITIOUS AND EASY RECIPES TO
NOURISH YOUR SOUL

DR APARNA PRINJA & SHITAL SHAH

Dedications

To our beloved grandparents and parents
who empowered us

and

to our daughters, Anushri, Ananya, Aisha and Anjali
– this is for you.

Preface

Against the backdrop of a marked increase in the number of vegans and people experiencing allergies and intolerances, plus the overriding interest in improved nutrition, plant-based milks have witnessed a surge in popularity and consumption.

Two friends with a shared interest in encouraging healthy dietary habits, Aparna Prinja, a doctor and nutritionist, and Shital Shah, a private catering entrepreneur, have collaborated on this vibrant and energising book, Plant Milk Power.

This book provides easy and speedy recipes for homemade plant-based milks that are intended for everyone. Whether it is a quick and healthy breakfast for individuals leading a hectic lifestyle, or those interested in non-animal foods, this book beautifully reinforces the need for fresh and natural ingredients to revitalise the body every day.

The detailed information about the raw ingredients used, including their documented allergens, provides an invigorating and authoritative foundation. The authors' meticulous research debunks the common misperceptions about the lack of nutrients in plant-based milks. They have defined the natural sugars, fibre, protein, fats, vitamins, minerals and phytonutrients contained in the core ingredients. References to the healing properties of the ingredients and their usage in diverse cultures through the centuries are equally enlightening.

The recipes document the usage of the raw ingredients in a way that complements the advantages while compensating for some inherent deficiencies in each of them. For example, the recipes suggest an optional addition of a pinch of kelp to enhance the iodine content without distorting the flavour. Likewise, they use a limited quantity of dates, instead of refined sugar, to sweeten the milks. The extensive health benefits coupled with the notes and cautions make the recipes personalised to one's nutritional balance and physiological needs.

The streamlined process for executing the recipes takes the tedium out of making a breakfast or nutritious beverage for people from all walks of life. Whether you have never tasted a plant-based milk before, want to make them fresh at home, or are discovering the wealth of natural treasures, this book aims to give you the inspiration and know-how to experiment with and enjoy a whole new world of nutrition and flavour. If you are a perpetually wired professional, a student, an exhausted parent, self-employed or a home-based carer, this book was written with you in mind. Enjoy the recipes to learn how to nurture new habits, tantalise your taste buds and reinstate the equilibrium in your busy, daily life.

The productivity of the recipes, the depth of data, the colourful images, ingredients and efficiency of the swift preparations empowers you all to charge your day.

Contents

Seeds

Hemp Seeds

Pumpkin Seeds

Sesame Seeds

Sunflower Seeds

Coconut, Oat & Tiger Nut

Coconuts

Oats

Tiger Nuts

Compotes & Power Mix

Nuts

Almond blossom, sent to teach us
that the spring days will soon reach us.

Edwin Arnold

In our almond milks we have used eight almonds per recipe. We wanted to keep the amount of nuts used to the minimum needed to make a tasty milk. This is so that the nut content does not overload the digestive capacity of the body.

Almond Milk

8 almonds (about 12g), soaked in 60ml water overnight

2 dates, pitted

¼ tsp vanilla powder, paste or seeds from a pod

Pinch of kelp powder (optional)

220ml water

Remove the almonds from the water used to soak them in. Add the almonds, dates, vanilla, kelp (if using) and 220ml of fresh water to a high-powered blender. Blend until a smooth milk forms.

Variations

For a blueberry or raspberry and almond smoothie, add 150g of blueberries or raspberries to the ingredients before blending as above. (Makes 375ml)

For a cacao and almond milk, add half to one teaspoon of cacao powder or nibs to the ingredients before blending as above. (Makes 255ml)

For a peach and almond smoothie, add two ripe peaches (about 190g) to the ingredients before blending as above. (Makes 400ml)

To make any of the above into chia bowls, soak 15g of chia seeds in 60ml water overnight. Add the chia seeds, including the water they were soaked in, to the milk or smoothie and stir well to remove any clumps.

Adding chia seeds to the milk thickens it, since they have the unusual quality of becoming gelatinous when soaked in liquid. The result creates a lovely consistency for a breakfast smoothie full of calcium.

Blackberry, Chia and Almond Smoothie

8 almonds (about 12g), soaked in 60ml water overnight

10g chia seeds, soaked in 60ml water overnight

150g blackberries

2 dates, pitted

¼ tsp vanilla powder, paste or seeds from a pod

Pinch of kelp powder (optional)

110ml water

Remove the almonds from the water used to soak them in. Add the almonds, chia seeds, including the water they were soaked in, blackberries, dates, vanilla, kelp (if using) and 110ml of fresh water to a high-powered blender. Blend until a deep-magenta coloured smoothie is formed.

Variation

For a plum, chia and almond smoothie, replace the blackberries with 350g of ripe plums. Stone the plums and add to the ingredients before blending as above. This makes enough for two servings. (Makes 540ml)

Like almonds and chia seeds, mangoes contain healthy amounts of dietary fibre, vitamins and minerals. This bowl of goodness packs a real punch in terms of nutrition as well as being sweet and juicy.

Mango and Almond Chia Bowl

8 almonds (about 12g), soaked in 60ml water overnight

2 ripe mangoes (around 260g)

2 dates, pitted

Pinch of kelp powder (optional)

½ tsp ground ginger

1 lime, juiced

15g chia seeds, soaked in 60ml water overnight

Peel and dice the mango flesh. Remove the almonds from the water used to soak them in.

Add the almonds, mango flesh, dates, kelp (if using), ginger and lime juice to a high-powered blender and blend until a yellow smoothie is formed. You can add water to the smoothie for a thinner consistency if preferred.

Combine the mango smoothie with the chia seeds, including the water they were soaked in, and stir to remove any clumps.

Matcha means powdered in Japan, where it has been grown and used for centuries. It is a beautiful, vibrant green powder loaded with antioxidants.

Matcha, Chia and Almond Milk

8 almonds (about 12g), soaked in 60ml water overnight

10g chia seeds, soaked in 60ml water overnight

2 dates, pitted

¼ tsp vanilla powder, paste or seeds from a pod

½-1 tsp matcha green tea powder

220ml water

Remove the almonds from the water used to soak them in. Add the chia seeds, including the water they were soaked in, to a high-powered blender along with the almonds, dates, vanilla, matcha and 220ml of fresh water. Blend until you have a green milk.

Variation

For a raspberry, matcha and almond smoothie, add 150g of raspberries to the ingredients before blending as above. (Makes 370ml)

Moringa leaf powder is nutritious and packed with calcium. This tasty green milk needs only a few ingredients to whip up a really delicious breakfast you can enjoy on the go.

Moringa and Almond Milk

8 almonds (about 12g), soaked in 60ml water overnight

2 dates, pitted

¼ tsp vanilla powder, paste or seeds from a pod

1 tsp moringa leaf powder

220ml water

Remove the almonds from the water used to soak them in. Add the almonds, dates, vanilla, moringa and 220ml of fresh water to a high-powered blender. Blend until you have a smooth, green milk.

Variation

For a moringa and almond chia bowl, soak 15g of chia seeds in 60ml of water overnight. Add the chia seeds, including the water they were soaked in, to the milk. Stir well to remove any clumps and enjoy with fresh fruit or compote. (Makes 330ml | High calcium)

Serves 1 | Makes 270ml | Preparation time 5 minutes plus overnight soaking

Cashews make a delicious cream-coloured milk. Alternatively, you can delight in the flavoursome combination of cashew and chicory, which gives the milk a mellow coffee-like taste.

Cashew Nut Milk

6 cashews (about 9g), soaked in 60ml water overnight

2 dates, pitted

¼ tsp vanilla powder, paste or seeds from a pod

Pinch of kelp powder (optional)

200ml water

Remove the cashews from the water used to soak them in. Add the cashews, dates, vanilla, kelp (if using) and 200ml of fresh water to a high-powered blender and blend until a fine milk is formed.

Variations

For a chicory and cashew milk, add two teaspoons of powdered chicory to the ingredients before blending as above. (Makes 260ml)

To make a refreshing lemon and cashew milk, add the zest of half an unwaxed organic lemon to the ingredients before blending as above. (Makes 245ml)

Moringa leaf powder gives this cashew milk a nutritional boost. Cacao adds a velvety chocolate flavour, while blueberries or matcha give it a refreshing lift.

Moringa and Cashew Nut Milk

6 cashews (about 9g), soaked in 60ml water overnight

2 dates, pitted

¼ tsp vanilla powder, paste or seeds from a pod

½-1 tsp moringa leaf powder

200ml water

Remove the cashews from the water used to soak them in. Add the cashews, dates, vanilla, moringa and 200ml of fresh water to a high-powered blender. Blend until a fine milk is formed.

Variations

For a blueberry, moringa and cashew smoothie, add 150g of blueberries to the ingredients and reduce the amount of fresh water added to 100ml. (Makes 280ml)

For a cacao, moringa and cashew milk, add 1 heaped teaspoon of cacao powder to the ingredients before blending. (Makes 270ml)

For a matcha and cashew milk, replace the moringa with the same amount of matcha green tea powder and add to the ingredients before blending. (Makes 270ml)

To make any of the above into chia bowls, soak 15g of chia seeds in 60ml of water overnight. Add the chia seeds, including the water they were soaked in, to the milk or smoothie and stir well to remove any clumps. (High calcium)

Serves 1 | Makes 270ml | Preparation time 5 minutes plus overnight soaking

The sweet and floral combination of raspberry and rosewater lends the chia bowl variation of this smoothie its 'Turkish Delight' nickname. Rose is a signature flavour for the traditional Turkish confection.

Raspberry and Cashew Nut Smoothie

6 cashews (about 9g), soaked in 60ml water overnight

150g fresh raspberries

2 dates, pitted

Pinch of kelp powder (optional)

1 tsp rosewater

½ unwaxed organic lemon, zested

110ml water

Remove the cashews from the water used to soak them in. Add the cashews, raspberries, dates, kelp (if using), rosewater, lemon zest and 110ml of fresh water to a high-powered blender. Blend until a smoothie is formed.

Variation

For a 'Turkish Delight' chia bowl, soak 15g of chia seeds in 60ml of water overnight. Add the chia seeds, including the water used to soak them in, to the smoothie and stir well to remove any clumps. (Makes 385ml)

Serves 1 | Makes 300ml | Preparation time 5 minutes plus overnight soaking

The fusion of strawberry, chia and cashew makes this the perfect summer smoothie! Depending on the sweetness of the strawberries, you may want to reduce the quantity of dates used.

Strawberry, Chia and Cashew Nut Smoothie

6 cashews (about 9g), soaked in 60ml water overnight

10g chia seeds, soaked in 60ml water overnight

200g fresh strawberries

2 dates, pitted

¼ tsp vanilla powder, paste or seeds from a pod

Pinch of kelp powder (optional)

100ml water

Remove the cashews from the water used to soak them in. Add the cashews, chia seeds, including the water they were soaked in, strawberries, dates, vanilla, kelp (if using) and 100ml of fresh water to a high-powered blender and blend until a smoothie is formed. Add more water if required to get the correct consistency.

Variation

For a raspberry, chia and cashew nut smoothie, replace the strawberries with 150g of raspberries and make the smoothie as above. Blend, making sure all the raspberry seeds are pulverised. (Makes 340ml)

Serves 1 | Makes 400ml | Preparation time 5 minutes plus overnight soaking

Hazelnuts produce a tasty and versatile milk. Adding chia seeds enhances the nutritional content of this flavoursome milk.

Hazelnut Milk

10 raw hazelnuts with skins (10g), soaked in 60ml water overnight

2 dates, pitted

¼ tsp vanilla powder, paste or seeds from a pod

Pinch of kelp powder (optional)

220ml water

Remove the hazelnuts from the water used to soak them in. Add the hazelnuts, dates, vanilla, kelp (if using) and 220ml of fresh water to a high-powered blender. Blend until the hazelnut skins are broken down and a fine milk is formed.

Alternatively, if you prefer a finer milk, remove the hazelnuts from the water used to soak them in. Combine the hazelnuts with 220ml of fresh water in a high-powered blender and blend. Sieve the milk using a muslin cloth, fine sieve or nut bag. Add the dates, vanilla and kelp (if using) to the sieved hazelnut milk and blend until a fine milk is formed.

Variation

For a chia and hazelnut milk, soak 10g of chia seeds in 60ml of water overnight. Combine the chia seeds, including the water they were soaked in, with the ingredients as above and blend to make a slightly granular milk. (Makes 330ml)

Alternatively, if sieving the hazelnut milk, add the chia seeds, including the water they were soaked in, to the sieved hazelnut milk. Next add the dates, vanilla and kelp (if using), then blend as above.

Serves 1 | Makes 260ml | Preparation time 5 minutes plus overnight soaking

It is easy to pair hazelnuts with many fruits and flavourings according to personal taste. Try swapping your morning coffee for the healthier alternative of a chicory and hazelnut smoothie.

Cacao, Chia and Hazelnut Smoothie

10 raw hazelnuts (10g) with skins, soaked in 60ml water overnight

20g chia seeds, soaked in 60ml of water overnight

2 dates, pitted

¼ tsp vanilla powder, paste or seeds from a pod

Pinch of kelp powder (optional)

1 tsp cacao powder or nibs

220ml water

Remove the hazelnuts from the water used to soak them in. Add all the ingredients, including the water used to soak the chia seeds in, to a high-powered blender. Blend until a smoothie is formed.

Variations

For a banana, cacao, chia and hazelnut smoothie, add one peeled ripe banana to the ingredients before blending as above. This variation serves one to two people. (Makes 440ml)

For a chicory, cacao, chia and hazelnut smoothie, add one to two teaspoons of chicory powder to the ingredients before blending as above. This gives the smoothie a mocha flavour. (Makes 330ml)

For an orange, cacao, chia and hazelnut smoothie, add the zest of half an unwaxed organic orange to the ingredients before blending as above. (Makes 330ml)

Serves 1 | Makes 330ml | Preparation time 5 minutes plus overnight soaking

The pistachio tree is a member of the cashew family. This luxurious milk works well with cardamom and rosewater, producing an exotic flavourful milk.

Pistachio Milk

20g shelled, raw, unsalted pistachios, soaked in 60ml water overnight

2 dates, pitted

¼ tsp vanilla powder, paste or seeds from a pod

Pinch of kelp powder (optional)

220ml water

Remove the pistachios from the water used to soak them in. Add the pistachios, dates, vanilla, kelp (if using) and 220ml of fresh water to a high-powered blender and blend until a fine milk is formed.

Variations

For a cardamom, rosewater and pistachio milk, add two cardamom pods and one teaspoon of rosewater to the ingredients and then blend as above. (Makes 260ml)

To make any of above milks into chia bowls, soak 30g of chia seeds in 70ml of water overnight. Add the chia seeds, including the water they were soaked in, to the milk and stir well to remove any clumps. (High calcium)

Revitalise the body with this simple chia and pistachio milk. For added flavour and colour, try the cacao, mango and raspberry variations.

Chia and Pistachio Milk

20g shelled, raw, unsalted pistachios, soaked in 60ml water overnight

15g chia seeds, soaked in 60ml water overnight

2 dates, pitted

¼ tsp vanilla powder, paste or seeds from a pod

Pinch of kelp powder (optional)

220ml water

Remove the pistachios from the water used to soak them in. Add all the ingredients, including the water used to soak the chia seeds, to a high-powered blender and blend until a thick but fine textured milk is formed.

Variations

For a cacao, chia and pistachio milk, add one teaspoon of cacao powder or nibs to the ingredients before blending as above. (Makes 325ml)

For a cardamom, mango, chia and pistachio smoothie, add one peeled and diced mango and two cardamom pods to the ingredients before blending as above. This variation serves one to two people. (Makes 585ml)

For a raspberry, chia and pistachio smoothie, add 200g of raspberries to the ingredients before blending as above. This variation serves one to two people. (Makes 465ml)

Serves 1 | Makes 325ml | Preparation time 5 minutes plus overnight soaking

Walnut milk blends well with a range of flavours, elevating their taste. It is a surprisingly sweet milk on its own and a firm favourite of ours!

Walnut Milk

4 walnut halves (about 11g), soaked in 60ml water overnight

2 dates, pitted

¼ tsp vanilla powder, paste or seeds from a pod

Pinch of kelp powder (optional)

220ml water

Remove the walnuts from the water used to soak them in. Add the walnuts, dates, vanilla, kelp (if using) and 220ml of fresh water to a high-powered blender and blend until a smooth milk forms.

Variations

For a cardamom, pistachio and walnut milk, soak 20g of raw unsalted pistachios in 60ml of water overnight. Remove the pistachios from the water used to soak them in. Next add the pistachios and two cardamom pods to the ingredients before blending. (Makes 290ml)

For a cherry and walnut milk, add 200g of fresh pitted cherries to the ingredients before blending. This variation serves one to two people. (Makes 435ml)

For a chicory and walnut milk, add one to two teaspoons of chicory to the ingredients before blending. (Makes 265ml)

For an orange and walnut milk, add the zest of half an unwaxed organic orange and two teaspoons of orange blossom water to the ingredients before blending. (Makes 265ml)

For chia bowls, soak 15g of chia seeds in 60ml of water overnight. Stir the chia seeds, including the water used to soak them in, to any of the above milks.

Serves 1 | Makes 265ml | Preparation time 5 minutes plus overnight soaking

This recipe uses almonds and walnuts. Savour the mocha flavour of this indulgent milk. For variety, use orange zest – it gives the milk a refreshing twist.

Almond, Cacao, Chicory and Walnut Milk

4 walnut halves (about 11g), soaked in 60ml water overnight

8 almonds (about 12g), soaked in 60ml water overnight

2 dates, pitted

¼ tsp vanilla paste, powder or seeds from a pod

Pinch of kelp powder (optional)

½ tsp cacao powder

1-2 tsp chicory powder

220ml water

Remove the walnuts and almonds from the water used to soak them in. Add the walnuts, almonds, dates, vanilla, kelp (if using), cacao, chicory and 220ml of fresh water to a high-powered blender. Blend until a smooth, chocolate-coloured milk is formed.

Variation

For an almond, cacao, orange and walnut milk, replace the chicory with the zest of half an unwaxed organic orange and blend as above. (Makes 275ml)

This straightforward recipe lends itself well to the comforting flavours of cacao and orange, or cardamom and rose.

Chia and Walnut Milk

4 walnut halves (about 11g), soaked in 60ml water overnight

10g chia seeds, soaked in 60ml water overnight

2 dates, pitted

¼ tsp vanilla powder, paste or seeds from a pod

Pinch of kelp powder (optional)

220ml water

Remove the walnuts from the water used to soak them in. Add the walnuts, chia seeds, including the water used to soak them in, dates, vanilla, kelp (if using) and 220ml of fresh water to a high-powered blender. Blend until a smooth milk forms.

Variations

For a cacao, orange, chia and walnut milk, add one teaspoon of cacao powder and the zest of half an unwaxed organic orange to the ingredients before blending as above. (Makes 350ml)

For a cardamom, rose, chia and walnut milk, add one teaspoon of rosewater and two cardamom pods to the ingredients before blending as above. (Makes 350ml)

Energise your day with this vibrant milk. For a more substantial breakfast, try the matcha and walnut chia bowl.

Matcha and Walnut Milk

4 walnut halves (about 11g), soaked in 60ml water overnight

2 dates, pitted

¼ tsp vanilla powder, paste or seeds from a pod

½-1 tsp matcha green tea powder

220ml water

Remove the walnuts from the water used to soak them in. Add the walnuts, dates, vanilla, matcha and 220ml of fresh water to a high-powered blender. Blend the ingredients together until a smooth, green milk forms.

Variation

For a matcha and walnut chia bowl, soak 15g of chia seeds in 60ml of water overnight. Stir the chia seeds, including the water they were soaked in, into the milk. Enjoy on its own, with fresh fruit or with fruit compote. (Makes 345ml)

Serves 1 | Makes 265ml | Preparation time 5 minutes plus overnight soaking

Seeds

To see things in the seed, that is genius.

Lao Tzu

These small seeds are a powerhouse of nutrients, protein, fibre and healthy fats. The use of dates, vanilla and citrus flavours mask the otherwise mild grassy taste.

Hemp Milk

50g unhulled hemp seeds, soaked in 60ml water overnight

220ml water

2 dates, pitted

¼ tsp vanilla powder, paste or seeds from a pod

Pinch of kelp powder (optional)

Sieve the hemp seeds to remove the water they were soaked in. Add the hemp seeds and 220ml fresh water to a high-powered blender and blend for 2 minutes.

Pour the milk through a sieve, muslin cloth or nut bag into a glass container.

Place the sieved milk back into the blender along with the dates, vanilla and kelp (if using) and blend until you have a smooth milk.

Variation

For a citrus-flavoured hemp milk, add the zest of half an unwaxed organic orange or lemon at the same time as the dates, vanilla and kelp (if using). (Makes 290ml)

Serves 1 | Makes 290ml | Preparation time 10 minutes plus overnight soaking

This nutritious smoothie brings together the classic combination of banana and chocolate. It is a great way to start the day!

Banana, Cacao and Hemp Smoothie

50g unhulled hemp seeds, soaked in 60ml water overnight

220ml water

1 ripe banana, peeled

2 dates, pitted

¼ tsp vanilla powder, paste or seeds from a pod

Pinch of kelp powder (optional)

½ tsp cacao powder or nibs

Sieve the hemp seeds to remove the water they were soaked in. Add the hemp seeds and 220ml fresh water to a high-powered blender and blend for 2 minutes.

Pour the milk through a sieve, muslin cloth or nut bag into a glass container.

Place the sieved milk back into the blender along with the banana, dates, vanilla, kelp (if using) and cacao.
Blend again to make a smoothie.

Variation

For a hazelnut, banana, cacao and hemp smoothie, soak 10 raw hazelnuts with skins on (about 10g) in 60ml of water overnight. Remove the hazelnuts from the water used to soak them in. Add the nuts to the hemp milk along with the dates, vanilla, kelp (if using), cacao and banana. Blend as above. (Makes 370ml)

Often lauded as a superfood, blueberries are nutritionally dense. They also taste delicious, especially when paired with sweet almonds and the uplifting zing of lemon zest.

Blueberry, Lemon, Almond and Hemp Smoothie

50g unhulled hemp seeds, soaked in 60ml water overnight

220ml water

8 almonds, soaked in 60ml water overnight

150g blueberries

2 dates, pitted

¼ tsp vanilla powder, paste or seeds from a pod

Pinch of kelp powder (optional)

½ organic unwaxed lemon or lime, zested

Sieve the hemp seeds to remove the water they were soaked in. Add the hemp seeds and 220ml of fresh water to a high-powered blender and blend for 2 minutes.

Pour the milk through a sieve, muslin cloth or nut bag into a glass container.

Remove the almonds from the water used to soak them in. Next add the almonds to the hemp milk with the blueberries, dates, vanilla, kelp (if using) and lemon or lime zest. Blend to form a smoothie.

Serves 1 | Makes 480ml | Preparation time 10 minutes plus overnight soaking

The small edible green seeds of the pumpkin are high in healthy fats and protein. They taste especially delicious when combined with the intense flavour of cacao and sweet raspberries.

Cacao, Raspberry, Chia and Pumpkin Seed Smoothie

20g pumpkin seeds, soaked in 60ml water overnight

10g chia seeds, soaked in 60ml water overnight

150g raspberries

2 dates, pitted

½ tsp vanilla powder, paste or seeds from a pod

Pinch of kelp powder (optional)

1 heaped tsp cacao powder or nibs

180ml water

Add the pumpkin seeds and chia seeds, including the water they were soaked in, to a high-powered blender along with the raspberries, dates, vanilla, kelp (if using), cacao and 180ml of fresh water. Blend all the ingredients together to form a smoothie.

Serves 1-2 | Makes 475ml | Preparation time 5 minutes plus overnight soaking

Walnuts add a depth of flavour to pumpkin and chia seeds, making this a nutrient-rich and sophisticated smoothie.

Walnut, Chia and Pumpkin Seed Smoothie

10g pumpkin seeds, soaked in 60ml water overnight

4 walnut halves, (11g) soaked in 60ml water overnight

10g chia seeds, soaked in 60ml water overnight

2 dates, pitted

¼ tsp vanilla powder, paste or seeds from a pod

Pinch of kelp powder (optional)

180ml water

Remove the walnuts from the water used to soak them in. Add the pumpkin seeds and chia seeds, including the water they were soaked in, along with the walnuts, dates, vanilla, kelp (if using) and 180ml of fresh water to a high-powered blender. Blend to form a smoothie.

Variation

For a banana, walnut, chia and pumpkin seed smoothie, add one peeled ripe banana to the ingredients before blending as above. Add more water for a finer consistency if preferred. (Makes 390ml)

Serves 1 | Makes 375ml | Preparation time 5 minutes plus overnight soaking

This lightly spiced milk can be jazzed up with refreshing orange, fragrant rose or sweet almonds and is very high in calcium no matter which variation you go for.

Sesame Seed Milk

15g unhulled sesame seeds, soaked in 60ml water overnight

2 cardamom pods

2 dates, pitted

¼ tsp vanilla powder, paste or seeds from a pod

¼ tsp ground cinnamon

Pinch of kelp powder (optional)

160ml water

Add the sesame seeds, including the water used to soak them in, and the cardamom, dates, vanilla, cinnamon, kelp (if using) and 160ml of fresh water to a high-powered blender. Blend until a smooth milk is formed.

Variations

For an almond and sesame seed milk, soak eight almonds (about 12g) in 60ml of water overnight. Remove the almonds from the water used to soak them in. Add the almonds to the rest of the ingredients, replacing cinnamon with a pinch of saffron, and blend as above. (Makes 270ml)

For a cacao, rose, pistachio and sesame seed milk, soak 15g of raw, shelled, unsalted pistachios in 60ml of water overnight. Remove the pistachios from the water used to soak them in. Add the pistachios to the rest of the ingredients, replacing cinnamon with one teaspoon of cacao powder or nibs and one teaspoon of rosewater. Blend as above. (Makes 290ml)

For an orange and sesame seed milk, replace the cinnamon with one teaspoon of orange blossom water and the zest of half an unwaxed organic orange. Blend as above. (Makes 270ml)

Create this easy revitalising milk which gives a refreshing boost to any morning.

Matcha, Almond and Sesame Seed Milk

10g unhulled sesame seeds, soaked in 60ml water overnight

8 almonds (about 12g), soaked in 60ml water overnight

2 dates, pitted

¼ tsp vanilla powder, paste or seeds from a pod

½-1 tsp matcha powder

160ml water

Remove the almonds from the water used to soak them in. Add the sesame seeds, including the water used to soak them in, to a high-powered blender along with the almonds, dates, vanilla, matcha and 160ml of fresh water. Blend until a fine, green milk is formed.

Serves 1 | Makes 270ml | Preparation time 5 minutes plus overnight soaking

The dried and ground leaf of the moringa plant significantly increases the nutrient content of this earthy milk.

Moringa, Cacao, Cashew Nut and Sesame Seed Milk

10g unhulled sesame seeds, soaked in 60ml water overnight

6 cashews (about 9g), soaked in 60ml water overnight

2 cardamom pods

2 dates, pitted

¼ tsp vanilla powder, paste or seeds from a pod

½ level tsp moringa leaf powder

1 heaped tsp cacao powder or nibs

1 tsp rosewater

160ml water

Remove the cashews from the water used to soak them in. Add the sesame seeds, including the water used to soak them in, to a high-powered blender along with the cashews, cardamom, dates, vanilla, moringa, cacao, rosewater and 160ml of fresh water. Blend until a smooth milk is formed.

Variation

For a banana, moringa, cacao, cashew nut and sesame seed milk, replace the rosewater with one peeled ripe banana and blend as above. (Makes 440ml)

The combination of pistachio, rose and sesame is reminiscent of the delectable Middle Eastern sweet halva. The inclusion of moringa elevates the nutrient and calcium content of this emerald-coloured milk.

Moringa, Pistachio, Rose and Sesame Seed Milk

15g unhulled sesame seeds, soaked in 60ml water overnight

15g shelled, raw, unsalted pistachios, soaked in 60ml water overnight

2 cardamom pods

2 dates, pitted

¼ tsp vanilla powder, paste or seeds from a pod

½ tsp moringa leaf powder

1 tsp rosewater

160ml water

Remove the pistachios from the water used to soak them in. Add the sesame seeds, including the water used to soak them in, to a high-powered blender. Add the pistachios, cardamom, dates, vanilla, moringa, rosewater and 160ml fresh water. Blend until a smooth green milk forms.

The tart flavour of baobab powder, which is rich in Vitamin C, really complements this nutrient-dense calcium punch.

Baobab, Cacao, Almond, Chia and Sesame Seed Calcium Punch

10g unhulled sesame seeds, soaked in 60ml water overnight

8 almonds (about 12g), soaked in 60ml water overnight

10g chia seeds, soaked in 60ml water overnight

2 dates, pitted

¼ tsp vanilla powder, paste or seeds from a pod

1 tsp baobab powder

1 tsp cacao powder or nibs

150ml water

Remove the almonds from the water used to soak them in. Add the sesame and chia seeds, including the water used to soak them in, to a high-powered blender. Next add the almonds, dates, vanilla, baobab, cacao and 150ml of fresh water. Blend until a thick smoothie is formed.

All the sesame seed recipes are high in calcium, but as the name suggests this one is a powerhouse of nutritional benefits, perfect before or after exercise.

Moringa, Almond, Chia and Sesame Seed Calcium Punch

10g unhulled sesame seeds, soaked in 60ml water overnight

8 almonds (about 12g), soaked in 60ml water overnight

10g chia seeds, soaked in 60ml water overnight

1 ripe banana, peeled

2 dates, pitted

¼ tsp vanilla powder, paste or seeds from a pod

½-1 tsp moringa leaf powder

200ml water

Remove the almonds from the water used to soak them in. Add the sesame and chia seeds, including the water used to soak them in, to a high-powered blender. Next add the almonds, banana, dates, vanilla, moringa and 200ml of fresh water. Blend until a thick smoothie is formed.

Serves 1-2 | Makes 475ml | Preparation time 5 minutes plus overnight soaking | High calcium

This is a nutritionally dense and nourishing milk, powered by a combination of seeds and pistachios.

Chia Nut and Seed Milk

20g sesame seeds

20g chia seeds

1 tsp sunflower seeds

1 tsp pumpkin seeds

15g shelled, raw, unsalted pistachios

3 cardamom pods

120ml water

2 dates, pitted

¼ tsp vanilla paste, powder or seeds from a pod

Pinch of kelp powder (optional)

1 tsp cacao powder or nibs

250ml water

Soak the sesame seeds, chia seeds, sunflower seeds, pumpkin seeds, pistachios and cardamom pods together in 120ml of water overnight.

The next day, place all the soaked ingredients, including the water they were soaked in, into a high-powered blender. Add the dates, vanilla, kelp (if using), cacao and 250ml of fresh water. Blend until a smooth milk is formed.

The unusual combination of rosewater and spices adds a delicate flavour to this nutrient-rich milk.

Linseed Nut and Seed Milk

20g sesame seeds

20g linseeds

1 tsp sunflower seeds

8 almonds (about 12g)

4 cardamom pods

120ml water

2 dates, pitted

¼ tsp vanilla paste, powder or seeds from a pod

Pinch of kelp powder (optional)

¼ tsp aniseed seeds

Generous pinch of saffron

1 tsp rosewater

200ml water

Soak the sesame seeds, linseeds, sunflower seeds, almonds and cardamom pods together in 120ml of water overnight.

The next day, place all the soaked ingredients, including the water they were soaked in, into a high-powered blender. To this, add the dates, vanilla, kelp (if using), aniseed, saffron, rosewater and 200ml of fresh water. Blend until a smooth milk is formed.

Serves 1 | Makes 400ml | Preparation time 5 minutes plus overnight soaking | High calcium

Sunflower seeds are readily available. This quick recipe, or any of the tasty variations, will stave off any mid-morning hunger pangs!

Sunflower Seed Milk

30g sunflower seeds, soaked in 60ml water overnight

2 dates, pitted

¼ tsp vanilla powder, paste or seeds from a pod

Pinch of kelp powder (optional)

180ml water

Add the sunflower seeds, including the water they were soaked in, to a high-powered blender along with the dates, vanilla, kelp (if using) and 180ml of fresh water. Blend until a fine milk is formed.

Variations

For an almond and sunflower seed milk, soak six almonds in 60ml of water overnight. Remove the almonds from the water used to soak them in. Add the almonds to the rest of the ingredients before blending as above. (Makes 310ml)

For a cacao, orange and sunflower seed milk, add the zest of half an unwaxed organic orange and one level teaspoon of cacao powder to the ingredients then blend as above. (Makes 310ml)

To make any of the above into chia bowls, soak 15g of chia seeds in 60ml of water overnight. Add the chia seeds, including the water they were soaked in, to the milk and stir well to remove any clumps.

Serves 1 | Makes 310ml | Preparation time 5 minutes plus overnight soaking

Coconut, Oat &
Tiger Nut

Don't quarrel with the coconut-palm climber:
the coconut has been eaten by the moon.

Swahili Proverb

This milk requires time and patience to make. The result is definitely worth the effort. Nothing quite beats the taste of this pure, white, glistening milk.

How To Make Coconut Milk

Holding the coconut in one hand, hammer around the circumference of the coconut using the blunt end of a large knife or a pestle.

Put the coconut in a clear bag and seal the bag. Throw the bag with the coconut inside it onto a hard floor until the outer shell of the coconut breaks.

Collect the water from inside the coconut and set aside. Remove the coconut flesh from the shell with the help of a butter knife and then cut the flesh into small pieces.

Weigh the coconut flesh and place in a high-powered blender. To this, add water. The amount of water required is twice the weight of the coconut flesh collected. This should include the coconut water collected and set aside earlier. For example, if the coconut flesh weighs 200g and 20ml of coconut water has been collected, add 380ml fresh water plus the 20ml coconut water collected to the coconut flesh. Blend together until a milk is formed.

Sieve the milk through a muslin cloth or nut bag into a jug. Place the flesh back into the blender, add 200 to 250ml water and blend again. Sieve this through the muslin cloth or nut bag into the jug containing the first lot of coconut milk. The coconut milk is now ready for use.

One coconut should yield approximately 500 to 700ml of coconut milk. Any extra milk can be stored in an airtight glass container and refrigerated for up to two days.

Serves 2 or more | Makes 500-700ml | Preparation time 30 minutes

Banana and coconut is a lovely tropical pairing that creates a rich, thick smoothie with a high fat and fibre content that keeps you feeling full.

Banana, Cacao and Coconut Smoothie

200ml coconut milk

1 ripe banana, peeled

15g chia seeds, soaked in 60ml water overnight

2 dates, pitted

¼ tsp vanilla paste, powder or seeds from a pod

Pinch of kelp powder (optional)

1 tsp cacao powder or nibs

Make the coconut milk as per the guide on page 78.

Blend the milk with the banana, chia seeds, including the water used to soak them in, the dates, vanilla, kelp (if using) and cacao in a high-powered blender until you have a velvety smoothie.

Serves 1 | Makes 360ml | Preparation time 30 minutes plus overnight soaking

This is an antioxidant-rich and nutritionally balanced milk. The addition of chia seeds gives the milk a thicker consistency.

Matcha, Chia and Coconut Milk

250ml coconut milk

15g chia seeds, soaked in 60ml water overnight

2 dates, pitted

¼ tsp vanilla paste, powder or seeds from a pod

1 heaped tsp matcha green tea powder

Make the coconut milk as per the guide on page 78.

Blend the milk with the chia seeds, including the water used to soak them in, dates, vanilla and matcha in a high-powered blender until you have a smooth green milk.

Experiment with rich coconut milk, aromatic vanilla, sweet dates and the unusual flavour of moringa leaf powder. The flavours are balanced and satisfying in this simple four-ingredient recipe.

Moringa and Coconut Milk

200ml coconut milk

2 dates, pitted

¼ tsp vanilla paste, powder or seeds from a pod

1 tsp moringa leaf powder

Make the coconut milk as per the guide on page 78.

Blend the milk with the dates, vanilla and moringa in a high-powered blender until you have a smooth green milk.

Variation

For a moringa and coconut chia bowl, soak 15g of chia seeds in 60ml of water overnight. Stir the chia seeds, including the water used to soak them in, into the moringa and coconut milk. Enjoy the chia bowl on its own or with fresh fruit. (High calcium)

Serves 1 | Makes 215ml | Preparation time 30 minutes plus overnight soaking

This is a warming and restorative milk. Gently toasting the turmeric before adding it to the milk draws out the flavour, giving the milk even more of an aromatic scent and taste.

Turmeric and Coconut Milk

250ml coconut milk

½-1 tsp turmeric powder

15g chia seeds, soaked in 60ml water overnight

2 cardamom pods

2 dates, pitted

¼ tsp vanilla paste, powder or seeds from a pod

Generous pinch of saffron

Make the coconut milk as per the guide on page 78.

Gently toast the turmeric in a dry pan over a low heat until it smells fragrant. This should take less than 1 minute.

Add the turmeric to the coconut milk along with the chia seeds, including the water they were soaked in, cardamom, dates, vanilla and saffron. Blend all the ingredients in a high-powered blender until you have a smooth golden milk.

If preferred, the milk can then be simmered gently and served warm.

Serves 1 | Makes 330ml | Preparation time 30 minutes plus overnight soaking

Oats are an ancient cereal grain with an impressive range of health benefits. Oat milks have become more and more popular in recent years. This is an easy recipe to make straight out of your kitchen!

Oat Milk

30g jumbo or rolled oats, soaked in 120ml water overnight

2 dates, pitted

¼ tsp vanilla powder, paste or seeds from a pod

Pinch of kelp powder (optional)

120ml water

Soak the oats in 120ml of water overnight – the oats will absorb all the water. Add all the ingredients to a high-powered blender. Blend until a smooth milk is formed. Add more water for a thinner milk if preferred.

Variations

For a banana, cacao and oat smoothie, add one peeled ripe banana and one teaspoon of cacao powder or nibs to the ingredients and blend as above. (Makes 390ml)

For a chicory and oat milk, add one to two teaspoons of chicory powder before blending all the ingredients together as above. This gives the oat milk a coffee-like flavour. (Makes 300ml)

To make any of the above into chia bowls, soak 15g of chia seeds in 60ml of water overnight. Add the chia seeds, including the water they were soaked in, to the milk or smoothie and stir well to remove any clumps.

Serves 1 | Makes 300ml | Preparation time 10 minutes plus overnight soaking

Colour your day with the delightful flavour of blueberries. Energise with this antioxidant-rich smoothie.

Blueberry and Oat Smoothie

30g jumbo or rolled oats, soaked in 120ml water overnight

150g blueberries

2 dates, pitted

¼ tsp vanilla powder, paste or seeds from a pod

Pinch of kelp powder (optional)

120ml water

Soak the oats in 120ml of water overnight – the oats will absorb all the water. Add all the ingredients to a high-powered blender and blend until you have a smoothie. Add more water for a thinner consistency if preferred.

Variations

For a raspberry and oat smoothie, replace the blueberries with 150g of raspberries and blend as above to make a pink smoothie. (Makes 450ml)

To make any of the above into chia bowls, soak 15g of chia seeds in 60ml of water overnight. Add the chia seeds, including the water they were soaked in, to the smoothie and stir well to remove any clumps.

Serves 2 | Makes 450ml | Preparation time 10 minutes plus overnight soaking

The addition of chia seeds to the moringa or matcha oat milk enriches this already high-antioxidant and nutritious beverage.

Moringa and Oat Milk

30g jumbo or rolled oats, soaked in 120ml water overnight

2 dates, pitted

¼ tsp vanilla powder, paste or seeds from a pod

1 level tsp moringa leaf powder

120ml water

Soak the oats in 120ml of water overnight – the oats will absorb all the water. Add all the ingredients to a high-powered blender and blend until a fine, green milk is formed. Add more water for a thinner consistency if preferred.

Variations

For a matcha and oat milk, replace the moringa with the same amount of matcha powder and blend as above. (Makes 300ml)

To make either of the above into chia bowls, soak 15g of chia seeds in 60ml of water overnight. Add the chia seeds, including the water they were soaked in, to the milk and stir well to remove any clumps. (High calcium)

Serves 1 | Makes 300ml | Preparation time 10 minutes plus overnight soaking

This nutrient-dense tuber makes an amazing milk that is free from dairy, gluten, nuts and seeds. As it is a naturally sweet milk, we have not added dates to this basic recipe.

Tiger Nut Milk

100g tiger nuts, soaked in 140ml water overnight

400ml water

¼ tsp vanilla paste, powder, or seeds from a pod

Pinch of kelp powder (optional)

Remove the tiger nuts from the water they were soaked in overnight. Add the tiger nuts and 400ml of fresh water to a high-powered blender. Blend for 2 minutes or until the tiger nuts are completely crushed.

Strain the milk through a fine sieve or pour into a muslin cloth or nut bag over a bowl or container. The fibrous part will remain in the sieve or cloth and the liquid will drip through to produce a sweet, white milk.

Add the vanilla, and kelp (if using), to the milk and blend again. Stir well before serving.

Variations

For a cardamom, lemon, rose and tiger nut milk, add one cardamom pod, the zest of half an unwaxed organic lemon and three quarters of a teaspoon of rosewater to the milk along with the vanilla and kelp (if using). Blend and stir as above. (Makes 350ml)

For an orange and tiger nut milk, add the zest of half an unwaxed organic orange to the milk along with the vanilla and kelp (if using). Blend and stir as above. (Makes 350ml)

To make any of the above into chia bowls, soak 30g of chia seeds in 70ml of water overnight. Add the chia seeds, including the water they were soaked in, to the milk and stir well to remove any clumps. Enjoy the bowl on its own or with the power mix, fresh fruit, compote or seeds.

Serves 1 | Makes 350ml | Preparation time 12 minutes plus overnight soaking

The deep flavour of black sesame seeds enhances the chocolatey taste of this already delicious pistachio and tiger nut milk.

Black Sesame, Cacao, Pistachio and Tiger Nut Milk

50g tiger nuts, soaked in 70ml water overnight

220ml water

15g shelled, raw, unsalted pistachio nuts, soaked in 60ml water overnight

10g black sesame seeds, soaked in 60ml water overnight

2 dates, pitted

¼ tsp vanilla paste, powder or seeds from a pod

Pinch of kelp powder (optional)

1 heaped tsp cacao powder or nibs

Ice cubes (optional)

Make the tiger nut milk recipe as described on page 94, using the 50g of tiger nuts and 220ml of fresh water.

Remove the pistachios from the water used to soak them in, and then add the pistachios to the tiger nut milk. Next add the black sesame seeds, including the water they were soaked in, to the milk along with the dates, vanilla, kelp (if using) and cacao.

Blend using a high-powered blender until you have a chocolate-coloured milk.

Add ice cubes (if using) and enjoy this rich, velvety chocolate milk.

Serves 1 | Makes 300ml | Preparation time 12 minutes plus overnight soaking

This warming and restorative milk is a nutrious alternative to the popular but often overly sugary chai lattes.

Chai Spiced Tiger Nut Milk

500ml water

3 black peppercorns

3 cardamom pods

2½cm (1 inch) stick of cinnamon or ½-1 tsp ground cinnamon

4g fresh ginger, peeled and roughly chopped

Generous pinch of saffron

100g tiger nuts, soaked in 140ml water overnight

8 almonds, (about 12g) soaked in 60ml water overnight

8 shelled, raw, unsalted pistachios, soaked in 60ml water overnight

2 dates, pitted

Pinch of kelp powder (optional)

1 tsp rosewater

Add 500ml of water, black peppercorns, cardamom pods, cinnamon, ginger and saffron to a saucepan and bring to the boil. Simmer for 15 minutes then remove the pan from the heat and set aside to cool, allowing the spices to infuse and flavour the water.

Once cooled, sieve the spiced water, retaining the liquid as a base for the tiger nut milk and keeping the spices for later.

Add enough hot water to the spiced water to make it up to 400ml. Blend this with the 100g of tiger nuts (removed from the water they were soaked in) and sieve the milk as described in the recipe on page 94.

Remove the almonds and pistachios from the water used to soak them in. Add the nuts, dates, kelp (if using), rosewater and the spices set aside earlier to the milk. Blend using a high-powered blender to make an aromatic spiced milk. Serve warm.

Serves 2 | Makes 450ml | Preparation time 40 minutes plus overnight soaking

The harmonious fusion of the flavours of matcha, chia and tiger nut creates this appetising milk.

Matcha, Chia and Tiger Nut Milk

50g tiger nuts, soaked in 70ml water overnight

220ml water

10g chia seeds, soaked in 60ml water overnight

2 dates, pitted

¼ tsp vanilla paste, powder or seeds from a pod

1 heaped tsp matcha powder

Make the tiger nut milk recipe as described on page 94, using the 50g of tiger nuts and 220ml of fresh water.

Add the chia seeds, including the water they were soaked in, to the milk along with the dates, vanilla and matcha. Blend using a high-powered blender until you have a fine green milk.

Serves 1 | Makes 310ml | Preparation time 12 minutes plus overnight soaking

This nutritious and enjoyable milk or chia bowl is a good way to start your day!

Moringa and Tiger Nut Milk

50g tiger nuts, soaked in 70ml water overnight

160ml water

2 dates, pitted

¼ tsp vanilla paste, powder or seeds from a pod

1 heaped tsp moringa leaf powder

Make the tiger nut milk recipe as described on page 94, using the 50g of tiger nuts and 160ml of fresh water.

Add the dates, vanilla and moringa to the milk. Blend using a high-powered blender until a fine green milk is formed.

Variation

For a moringa and tiger nut chia bowl, soak 10g of chia seeds in 60ml of water overnight. Add the chia seeds, including the water used to soak them in, to the moringa and tiger nut milk. Stir well to break up the chia clumps. (Makes 330ml | High calcium)

Serves 1 | Makes 225ml | Preparation time 12 minutes plus overnight soaking

A lovely, nutritionally dense and delectable smoothie. Depending on the sweetness of the fruits used, you can eliminate the dates from this recipe.

Raspberry and Tiger Nut Smoothie

50g tiger nuts, soaked in 70ml water overnight

200ml water

150g raspberries

10g chia seeds, soaked in 60ml water overnight

2 dates, pitted

¼ tsp vanilla paste, powder or seeds from a pod

Pinch of kelp powder (optional)

80ml water

Make the tiger nut milk recipe as described on page 94, using the 50g of tiger nuts and 200ml of fresh water.

Add the chia seeds, including the water used to soak them in, as well as the raspberries, dates, vanilla, kelp (if using) and the additional 80ml of fresh water to the milk. Blend using a high-powered blender until you have a pink smoothie.

It is best to drink this smoothie fresh, as it can thicken quickly due to the chia seeds.

Variations

For a blackberry and tiger nut smoothie, replace the raspberries with 150g of blackberries and blend as above. (Makes 510ml)

For a blueberry and tiger nut smoothie, replace the raspberries with 125g of blueberries and blend as above. (Makes 490ml)

For a mango and tiger nut smoothie, replace the raspberries with one peeled and diced mango and blend as above. You can also add 5g of peeled and roughly chopped fresh ginger before blending for a more warming flavour. (Makes 505ml)

Serves 2 | Makes 480ml | Preparation time 12 minutes plus overnight soaking

Compotes &
Power Mix

Love is a fruit in season at all times,
and within reach of every hand.

Mother Teresa

If you want to make this compote a little sweeter, for children or those with a sweet tooth, you can add up to five more grapes. It keeps well in the fridge for up to three days.

Blueberry Compote

150g blueberries

5 red grapes (about 25g), liquidised

1 stick of cinnamon

½ vanilla pod

2 cloves

Place all the blueberries, the liquidised grapes, cinnamon stick, vanilla and cloves into a pan. Cook over a medium heat and stir gently until the liquid is a little syrupy and the blueberries are halfway between soft and firm. Remove the cinnamon stick, cloves and vanilla pod from the compote before serving. Add to a chia bowl or spoon over porridge for a delicious breakfast.

Variations

For a blackberry compote, replace the blueberries with the same quantity of blackberries and follow the method above.

For a raspberry compote, replace the blueberries with the same quantity of raspberries and follow the method above.

Serves 1-2 | Preparation time 5 minutes plus cooking time

This compote is lovely added either to chia bowls or your morning porridge. It can be made sweeter or sharper according to your preference and depending on the variety of apples or pears used.

Steamed Apple Compote

4 tbsp water

2 small apples, cored and diced

In a saucepan heat the water until just boiling. Add the chopped apple, cover the pan with a lid and cook for 1 minute or until just softened.

Variation

For a steamed pear compote, replace the apples with one cored and diced pear and follow the method above.

This powder is high in protein and fibre; a multi-mineral and vitamin mix which augments a healthy breakfast.

Power Mix

1 tbsp linseeds

1 tbsp sesame seeds

½ tbsp pumpkin seeds

½ tbsp sunflower seeds

1 clove

2 cardamom pods

2½cm (1 inch) stick of cinnamon

Combine all the ingredients in a spice grinder and grind to a fine powder.

Sprinkle a teaspoon of the powder over milks, smoothies, porridge, chia bowls and granola. It could also be added to salads or soups.

Store in an airtight container in the fridge for up to 2 days.

Below is a general overview of things to be aware of when using this book.

About Our Ingredients

Allergies & Intolerances

An allergy is a reaction by the immune system to foods, dust, medication, pollen and other substances which can affect any part of the body. Allergic reactions can range from being very mild to severe and potentially life threatening. In contrast, a food intolerance involves the digestive system and is not life threatening.

If someone is allergic or intolerant to a particular ingredient, then they could also be allergic or intolerant to another member of the same plant family as follows:

Anacardiaceae family – includes cashews, mangoes, pistachios and poison ivy

Apiaceae family – includes anise, caraway, carrot, celery, coriander, cumin, dill, fennel and parsley

Arecaceae family – includes coconut, dates, jaggery, palm heart and palm oil

Asteraceae or Compositae family – includes chamomile, chicory, chrysanthemums, daisies, echinacea, marigolds, ragweed, tarragon and sunflower

Rosaceae family – includes almonds, apples, apricots, blackberries, cherries, peaches, pears, plums, raspberries, roses and strawberries

Please note:

Some people are also allergic or intolerant to more than one type of tree nut even though they may belong to different plant families.

If someone is allergic or intolerant to any of our ingredients, they should avoid them and consult with their physician before use.

Oxalates

People with calcium oxalate kidney stones who have been advised by their physician to follow a low oxalate diet should be aware that oxalates can be found in many food groups including:

Nuts – especially almonds and cashews

Fruits – especially berries, grapes, dates, lemon and orange peel

Seeds – especially sunflower and sesame

Cacao

Antioxidants

Antioxidants are substances such as Vitamins C and E, copper, selenium, zinc, manganese and carotenoids. These protect the body from the damaging effects of its own metabolism and the external environment. All the ingredients in this book contain quantities of beneficial antioxidants.

Nutritional Notes

The milks in this book contain good amounts of fibre, protein, healthy fats, vitamins and minerals. Vegans and vegetarians however, may need to supplement their diet with Vitamins D, B12 and K2.

To increase plant-based omega-3 oils in our milks we have used chia seeds and linseeds/flaxseeds.

To increase the calcium content in our milks, we have used chia seeds, moringa leaf powder and sesame seeds.

Buying, Preparing and Storing of Ingredients

Buy organic where possible to reduce exposure to pesticides and other chemicals, especially for fruits with thinner skins such as strawberries, apples and pears.

Wash all fruits, including dates, thoroughly before use to help reduce contamination by pesticides, other chemicals, bacteria and fungi.

Store nuts, seeds and spices in an airtight container and keep in a cool, dry place.

Soaking the nuts, seeds, oats and tiger nuts helps to soften them, hence making it easier to blend and digest them.

The following glossary of ingredients has been divided into three parts:

Core ingredients – These are the ingredients used to make the base milks.

Secondary ingredients – These are the signature flavourings used for their nutritional value.

Fruits – These are especially chosen for their health benefits and of course their flavours. They also complement the milks.

Almonds

Almonds (Prunus dulcis) are the edible seeds of the deciduous almond tree, which is thought to be native to parts of Asia and the Middle East. They are full of Vitamins E and B2 as well as minerals including manganese, magnesium, phosphorus and copper. Almonds contain healthy fats and protein with minimal sugar, and have plenty of fibre. The skins are rich in antioxidants which are thought to protect our body cells from damage. Anyone allergic to other members of the Rosaceae family could be allergic to almonds (see Allergies & Intolerances on page 116).

Cashews

These kidney-shaped seeds are a product of the evergreen tropical cashew tree (Anacardium occidentale) and are mainly produced in Brazil, India and African countries. Cashews contain mostly monounsaturated fats which are thought to be good for heart health. They also contain Vitamins E, B and K as well as minerals such as copper, manganese, magnesium and phosphorus. If eaten in excess, cashews can raise your blood sugar levels. Anyone allergic to other members of the Anacardiaceae family could be allergic to cashews (see Allergies & Intolerances on page 116).

Chia seeds

Chia seeds (Salvia hispanica) are tiny edible seeds that come in two varieties, black and white, both of which have the unusual quality of becoming gelatinous when soaked in liquid. Chia seeds are rich in omega-3 fatty acids and known for their anti-inflammatory effects in the body. They are a good source of dietary fibre, protein, calcium, magnesium and iron. Children, teenagers and those who have never eaten chia seeds before should start with very small quantities. Anyone pregnant, breastfeeding, taking any medication or with a medical condition should consult their physician before using chia seeds.

Coconuts

In countries such as India, coconuts (Cocos nucifera) are not only important for their culinary use but for cultural and religious rituals, for example as an offering in a temple or the smashing of a coconut at the start of a new project. The high fibre and fat content in coconut flesh is filling, while coconut water is a rehydrating mineral-rich drink. Young green coconuts contain more water and mature brown fibrous coconuts contain more coconut flesh. We have used mature coconuts in our recipes. Anyone allergic to other members of the Arecaceae family could be allergic to coconuts (see Allergies & Intolerances on page 116).

Hazelnuts

Hazelnuts (Corylus avellana) are thought to have originated from Asia. Today, Turkey is the largest commercial producer of hazelnuts. We have used whole, unroasted, unsalted hazelnuts in our recipes to boost the phytonutrient content of the milks. Hazelnuts contain Vitamins E, B1, B6 and folate as well as the minerals manganese, copper and magnesium. They also contain high amounts of protein, monounsaturated fats and fibre. Hazelnuts are low in sugar.

Hemp

Hemp (Cannabis sativa) has been cultivated for thousands of years for clothing, body care products, the automobile industry and food. Hemp seeds are high in fibre, very rich in protein and have a high healthy fat, Vitamin E and mineral content. It is important to note that marijuana comes from a different strain and contains a high percentage of tetrahydrocannabinol (THC) which is responsible for the psychoactive effect, whereas hemp seeds contain extremely low amounts of THC and are safe to eat. Anyone on blood thinning medication should consult their physician before using hemp.

Linseeds / Flax Seeds

Linseeds or flax seeds (Linum usitatissimum) have a high healthy fat content as well as being very rich in essential nutrients. Their high fibre content gives a feeling of fullness and supports digestive health, but eating too much may cause diarrhoea or bloating. Linseeds should always be taken with plenty of water. They should be stored in an airtight container in the fridge as they can oxidise quickly. Anyone pregnant, breast feeding or diagnosed with cancer, a bleeding disorder, diabetes, high blood pressure, or taking any medication and supplements should consult their physician before using linseeds.

Oats

Oats (Avena sativa) are an ancient cereal grain grown in many parts of the world. Oats are highly beneficial to health as they are a great source of protein, dietary fibre and complex carbohydrates. They give our bodies a sense of fullness and are thought to improve blood sugar regulation. Oats also retain water and support gut health. However, anyone with coeliac disease should avoid oats because of the risk of cross-contamination with wheat, rye or barley. Gluten-free oats are available for anyone in remission with coeliac disease, or for those who follow a gluten-free diet.

Pistachios

Pistachios (Pistacia vera) are thought to originate from Asia and the Middle East and are highly prized in the local cuisines there. We have used shelled, raw, unsalted pistachios in our recipes to increase the nutrient content of the milk, as there are plenty of health benefits to be gained from these tasty nuts. They contain Vitamins B6 and B1, copper, potassium, magnesium, iron and carotenoids. They are high in protein and fibre, and mostly monounsaturated fats. Pistachios are thought to support eye and heart health. Anyone allergic to members of the Anacardiaceae family could be allergic to pistachios (see Allergies & Intolerances on page 116).

Pumpkin Seeds

Pumpkins (Cucurbita pepo) originated from the Americas. The small green edible seeds (pepita) from this vegetable are highly nutritious and were valued amongst Native American tribes for both their culinary and medicinal properties. Pumpkin seeds contain small amounts of Vitamin B and E derivatives, manganese, phosphorus, copper, magnesium, zinc and iron. They are high in healthy fats, protein and fibre and contain very little sugar. The nutrients in pumpkin seeds are thought to support immunity, digestion, metabolism, heart and reproductive health. In our recipes, we have used raw unsalted pumpkin seeds.

Sesame Seeds

Sesame seeds come from the flowering sesame plant (Sesamum indicum) which is thought to have originated in India. Sesame seeds are highly nutritious and contain good amounts of Vitamin B1, copper, manganese, calcium, phosphorus, magnesium, iron, zinc, and selenium. They are a good source of protein, complex carbohydrates, fibre and healthy fats. We have used raw, unhulled, unsalted sesame seeds to increase the calcium content of our milks. Anyone on medication, herbs or supplements to treat diabetes or lower blood pressure should consult their physician before using sesame seeds.

Sunflower Seeds

Sunflowers (Helianthus annuus) are thought to have originated from Mexico and Peru. Sunflower seeds give a feeling of fullness thanks to a high level of protein, complex carbohydrates, fibre, and mono and polyunsaturated fats. They are packed with nutrients such as Vitamins E, B1, B6, folate, manganese, copper, magnesium, phosphorus, selenium, zinc and iron. We have used shelled, raw, unsalted sunflower seeds in our recipes. Anyone allergic to any flowers or herbs of the Asteraceae or Compositae family could be allergic to sunflower seeds (see Allergies & Intolerances on page 116).

Tiger Nuts

Tiger nuts (Cyperus esculentus) are thought to have originated in Ancient Egypt. Tiger nut milk is commonly drunk in Spain where it is used to make a sweet drink called horchata. This is a good milk to try if allergic to nuts and seeds, as tiger nuts are actually a dried edible tuber and produce a naturally sweet, nutritious milk. If eating tiger nuts for the first time, the high fibre content may cause some initial gas and bloating but will regulate bowel activity and give a feeling of fullness. They are also rich in protein, monounsaturated fats and complex carbohydrates.

Walnuts

Walnuts are the brain-shaped edible fruit of the walnut tree (Juglans regia) encased in a distinctive 'wrinkly' hard shell. These large nuts contain high levels of protein, fibre, and polyunsaturated fats. Vitamins B6, B1 and folate are also present alongside copper, manganese and magnesium. Walnuts are thought to support brain and heart health. They are low in sugars and give a feeling of fullness, so provide a great start to any day.

Anise/Aniseed

Anise, or aniseed, (Pimpinella anisum) are the small green seeds of a flowering plant which grows in Asia and the Mediterranean. Their warming, pungent and sweet flavour is similar to liquorice. Aniseed has traditionally been used as a mouth freshener. It contains Vitamins B6 and C as well as iron and manganese. Anyone with uterine fibroids, endometriosis or with hormone sensitive cancers such as breast, ovarian or uterine should avoid aniseed. Anyone allergic to other members of the Apiaceae family could be allergic to aniseed (see Allergies & Intolerances on page 116).

Baobab Powder

The baobab tree (Adansonia digitata) is an ancient species of very large tree native to Africa, Australia and the Middle East. The fruit, pulp and seeds are encased in a hard shell, which falls to the ground once ripe. To harvest the edible parts, the shell must be broken and the pulp, fibre and seeds are sieved and dried to produce a powder. Baobab powder is whitish-pink in colour and has a tart taste. It has a high Vitamin C content and is thought to support gut and skin health. Anyone pregnant or breast feeding should consult their physician before using baobab. In recipes where baobab has been used, kelp has not been included. This is because baobab may contain some iodine.

Cacao

Cacao (Theobroma cacao) is thought to have originated in Central America thousands of years ago. It is made by cold-pressing raw cacao beans to produce cacao butter and nibs. Cocoa is produced using roasted beans and therefore packs less of a nutritional punch. High in fibre with a bittersweet flavour, cacao also contains caffeine which is why eating too much can cause nausea, an increased pulse rate and headaches. In our recipes we have used a teaspoon of this mineral-rich food.

Cardamom (Green)

This is an ancient, green-coloured, fragrant spice prized in Asian cooking. Cardamom (Elettaria cardamomum) is part of the ginger (Zingiberaceae) family and is cultivated in India, Sri Lanka, Malaysia, Guatemala and parts of Africa. In our recipes we have included whole cardamom pods, which consist of an outer fibrous casing enclosing small black seeds. Cardamom is mostly complex carbohydrates and fibre, with very little protein and fat, and also contains the essential oil cineole. Cardamom is thought to support digestive health.

Chicory

Raw chicory root (Cichorium intybus) is a complex carbohydrate with good levels of fibre, particularly inulin, which is thought to support gut health. Roasted and powdered chicory is a great coffee substitute and is used in several of our milks. Anyone pregnant, breastfeeding, on any medications, herbs or supplements to control diabetes, or affected by gallstones should consult their physician before using chicory. Chicory should be avoided for two weeks prior to any elective surgery as it may lower blood sugar. Anyone allergic to other members of the Asteraceae or Compositae family could be allergic to chicory (see Allergies & Intolerances on page 116).

Cinnamon

Cinnamon (Cinnamomum aromaticum/verum) comes from the inner bark of an evergreen tree. It is grown mainly in Asia and South America and is an ancient aromatic spice with deep, warming and sweet tones. Cinnamon can be used to sweeten recipes without adding sugar and has been used as a food preservative. It is high in fibre and the mineral manganese. Anyone who is diabetic or has a liver disorder should consult their physician before using cinnamon. Cinnamon should be avoided for two weeks prior to any elective surgery as it may lower blood sugar.

Cloves

Cloves (Syzygium aromaticum) are the dried, unopened, pink flower buds of the clove tree. Cloves are a warming, pungent, aromatic ancient spice grown in Zanzibar, India, Indonesia, the West Indies, Sri Lanka, Madagascar and Brazil. They are thought to support the digestive system, and have been used traditionally to treat tooth and gum pain. Small amounts of Vitamins K, C, E and B6 are present in cloves as well as the minerals manganese, calcium, iron, magnesium and potassium.

Dates

Dates (Phoenix dactylifera) are the fibrous, sweet and succulent fruit of the date palm. In our recipes, we have used two medjool dates as they contain a good amount of calcium and sweeten the milks, especially for people used to eating a diet with more refined sugar. Reduce the quantity or eliminate dates from the recipe according to taste. Dates are a good source of fibre, Vitamins B6, K, A and the minerals potassium, manganese, copper, magnesium, iron, zinc and phosphorous. Anyone allergic to other members of the Arecaceae family could also be allergic to dates (see Allergies & Intolerances on page 116).

Ginger

Ginger root (Zingiber officinale) is a commonly used spice in Asian cuisine. Ginger is warming and aromatic with a distinctive spicy flavour. It has been used for thousands of years to support digestive, joint, respiratory and reproductive health. We have used both the fresh root and the dried powder in our recipes. Although ginger is safe in culinary amounts, eating too much can cause irritation in the mouth and throat, heartburn, or diarrhoea. Anyone pregnant or taking any medication, herbs or supplements for diabetes, thinning the blood or to control blood pressure should consult their physician before using ginger for a prolonged time period.

Kelp

Kelp is a seaweed belonging to the Phaeophyceae class of brown algae. It is full of vitamins and minerals, especially iodine. We have used a pinch of kelp powder to improve the iodine content of our milks. This is an optional ingredient and omitting it doesn't affect the taste. Before using kelp, anyone with a <u>thyroid disorder</u> should consult their physician as iodine could worsen hypothyroidism, hyperthyroidism and other thyroid conditions. Anyone pregnant, breastfeeding, taking medications, herbs or supplements to treat thyroid disease or thin the blood should consult their physician before using kelp. Kelp should be avoided two weeks prior to any elective surgery. Use organic, high quality kelp.

Maple Syrup

Maple syrup is the sap found in various varieties of maple trees in North America and Canada such as sugar maple (Acer saccharum), black maple (Acer nigrum) and red maple (Acer rubrum). It is a deep, golden brown, unrefined natural sweetener. Maple syrup is made up of mostly sugars and also contains several minerals including manganese, zinc, iron and potassium. If allergic to dates, we suggest replacing them with one teaspoon of maple syrup in our recipes.

Matcha Green Tea Powder

Matcha is a vibrant green powder made from steaming, drying and grinding the leaves of Camellia sinensis, a tea plant. This nutrient-rich, high protein powder is thought to support heart and brain health, boost metabolism, and enhance immunity. Green tea contains caffeine and if consumed in excess, matcha can cause constipation, an upset stomach, headaches, increased heart rate and anaemia. Pregnant women should be aware of the effects of caffeine on the foetus and limit their caffeine intake. Anyone on medication, herbs or supplements or who has a chronic illness should always consult their physician before using matcha green tea powder. In recipes where matcha has been used, kelp has not been included. This is because matcha may contain some iodine.

Moringa Leaf Powder

Moringa leaf powder (Moringa oleifera) is highly nutritious and rich in protein. It contains Vitamins A, C, K, E and some B vitamins as well as calcium, iron, magnesium, potassium, and zinc. Indigenous to India and Pakistan but now grown in many tropical parts of the world, the whole plant – root, stem, leaves, flowers, pods and seeds – can be used for cooking, or in Ayurvedic medicines. Anyone pregnant, breastfeeding or taking medications, herbs or supplements to control blood pressure, diabetes or treat hypothyroidism should consult their physician before using moringa leaf powder. In recipes where moringa has been used, kelp has not been included. This is because moringa may contain some iodine.

Peppercorns

Black pepper (Piper nigrum) is one of the world's most commonly used culinary spices and has been used in traditional medicine for centuries. Grown in India and South East Asia, it is the dried, fully grown, unripe fruit or berry of a flowering wood vine. These small round balls are high in fibre and contain Vitamin K and minerals such as manganese, potassium and iron. The active ingredient in peppercorns is piperine. Black pepper is safe when used in culinary amounts but using large amounts can cause a burning effect in the mouth and rest of the digestive tract.

Rosewater and Orange Blossom Water

We have used these delicate flavourings in some of our recipes to complement other ingredients and add distinctive floral or citrus notes. Rosewater (Rosa damascena) is made by steeping rose petals in water, or as a by-product of rose oil production which involves steam distillation. It is commonly used in Middle Eastern, Greek and Indian cuisine. It has been used in traditional medicine for its anti-inflammatory properties to help with skin disorders such as eczema. Orange blossom water (Citrus aurantium) is made through the distillation of bitter orange blossoms in North Africa, Europe, the Middle East and the USA.

Saffron

Saffron (Crocus sativus) is an ancient aromatic spice and one of the most expensive in the world. Saffron is cultivated and harvested by hand in Iran, Western Europe, Kashmir and China; the threads are obtained from the stigmas and styles of the flower. It contains safranal, a volatile oil that gives saffron its distinctive aroma. In our recipes we have used a pinch of saffron, as small amounts are safe in culinary use. High doses of 5g or more can be toxic. Anyone pregnant, or taking any medications, herbs and supplements for blood pressure or blood thinning should consult their physician before using saffron.

Turmeric

Turmeric (Curcuma longa) comes from a flowering plant in the ginger family which is grown in Asia, Africa and Australasia. The rhizomes are dried and ground to produce a bright yellow powder. This has a warm, bitter taste and contains the active ingredient curcumin. This powerful culinary spice has been used in traditional medicine for thousands of years to promote digestive, joint, and skin health. Turmeric is thought to be safe when used in culinary amounts. Anyone on any medication, herbs or supplements to control diabetes, thin the blood, or affected by gallstones should consult their physician before using turmeric therapeutically. Turmeric should be avoided for two weeks prior to any elective surgery.

Vanilla

The seeds and extract of vanilla (Vanilla planifolia) have a lovely flavour and aroma which enhances the taste of food. The pods come from a type of orchid grown in Madagascar, Uganda, India, Mexico, Indonesia and the West Indies. Vanilla is highly prized and is thought to be the second most expensive spice used in the culinary world. In our recipes we use vanilla in three forms: pure vanilla powder, which is made from grinding the vanilla bean; vanilla pods, using both the seeds found inside the pod and the pod itself; and vanilla bean paste, which is made from blended vanilla seeds.

Apples

Apples (Malus domestica) belong to the Rosaceae family and are the most commonly cultivated fruit worldwide. Apples contain high amounts of Vitamin C and fibre. The apple peel is also full of nutrients and insoluble fibre which supports gut health. Therefore, when eating an apple it is best to consume both the peel and the flesh. Avoid eating apple seeds in excess as they contain small amounts of hydrogen cyanide. Anyone allergic to birch tree pollen, or other members of the Rosaceae family could be allergic to apples (see Allergies & Intolerances on page 116).

Bananas

Bananas (Musa acuminata) come from a large flowering herbaceous plant, with leaves that can grow over three metres long. Bananas grow in tropical climates. The biggest producers of bananas today are India and China. They are rich in Vitamins B6 and C, and the minerals manganese and potassium. Bananas contain mostly carbohydrates, a good amount of fibre, low fat and some protein. Anyone taking medication, herbs or supplements for heart disease, blood pressure or kidney disease should consult their physician before eating bananas as they can increase potassium levels.

Blackberries

Blackberries (Rubus plicatus) are nutritionally dense, velvety black, juicy berries. Of all the berries, blackberries and raspberries have the highest calcium content. Like other berries they also contain flavonoids, compounds which are a source of their intense colour. Blackberries are thought to support brain, gut, heart and skin health and enhance immunity. Anyone allergic to other members of the Rosaceae family could be allergic to blackberries (see Allergies & Intolerances on page 116).

Blueberries

Blueberries (Vaccinium angustifolium) are grown all over the world in the wild, or are conventionally farmed. They contain Vitamins K and C and predominantly the mineral manganese. Amongst all the berries, blueberries have the highest antioxidant levels. They are thought to support brain, gut and heart health and may play a role in cancer prevention. Blueberries should be avoided for two weeks prior to any elective surgery. Anyone on any medication, herbs or supplements for diabetes, thinning the blood, or blood pressure should consult their physician before using blueberries therapeutically.

Cherries

Cherries are juicy stone fruits that come in two edible varieties, the sweet cherry (Prunus avium) and the sour cherry (Prunus cerasus), both from the Rosaceae family. Cherries are thought to support eye, gut, heart and joint health, enhance metabolism, aid sleep and may play a role in cancer prevention. They contain Vitamin C, potassium, calcium and fibre. It is best to buy organic where possible. Anyone allergic to other members of the Rosaceae family could be allergic to cherries (see Allergies & Intolerances on page 116).

Grapes

Grapes (Vitis vinifera) are part of the Vitaceae family and come in many different varieties. They contain Vitamins C and K, numerous phytonutrients and copper. Grapes are thought to support the heart and blood vessels, contribute to brain and eye health, reduce inflammation and have antimicrobial properties. The skin of grapes is full of nutrients and the seeds contain oils which can be used medicinally. In our compote recipes, we have used grapes with their skins on, and they do not have to be seedless as we have liquidised them before use.

Lemon Peel

Lemons (Citrus limon) are thought to have originated in Asia. Lemon peel is bright yellow in colour and has a bitter, sour taste with a refreshing aroma. It contains the essential oil limonene, Vitamin C and small amounts of the mineral calcium. The peel is made up of predominantly carbohydrates with lots of fibre. It is best to buy organic, unwaxed lemons where possible and always wash them before use as the peel may be covered in preservative wax and tends to retain pesticides.

Limes

Limes are hybrids of the citron (Citrus medica), mandarin orange (Citrus reticulata) and pomelo (Citrus maxima) fruits. They contain high levels of Vitamin C. In fact, limes were given to British sailors in the 18th century to prevent scurvy, a disease that was manifest due to Vitamin C deficiency. Limes are thought to support heart and skin health, enhance immunity, aid iron absorption, and may play a role in cancer prevention. It is best to buy organic limes where possible. Limes should always be eaten in moderation as the acid in limes can cause tooth erosion.

Mangoes

Mangoes (Mangifera indica) are thought to have originated from Asia and are now grown in tropical countries worldwide. They contain Vitamins C, A (and carotenoids), folate, B6 and E as well as minerals including copper, potassium, magnesium and manganese. Mangoes are thought to enhance immunity and support bone, brain, eye, hair, heart and skin health. Excessive consumption of mangoes can lead to diarrhoea. Anyone allergic to other members of the Anacardiaceae family could be allergic to mangoes (see Allergies & Intolerances on page 116).

Orange Peel

Sweet oranges (Citrus sinensis) are part of the Rutaceae family along with limes, lemons and many other citrus fruits. The orange peel can be green or bright orange and tastes bitter due to the essential oil limonene. Orange peel contains mainly Vitamin C and small amounts of the mineral calcium as well as phytonutrients. It is best to buy organic oranges where possible as the peel tends to retain pesticides. Always wash oranges before use. Note that excessive eating of orange peel by children may cause abdominal pain and affect their nervous system.

Peaches

The most commonly available peaches (Prunus persica) are spherical with yellow or white flesh, but there are flat varieties as well. Nectarines are actually a type of peach too. Peaches are thought to have originated in China where they are mostly grown today. They contain Vitamins C and A along with potassium, iron, zinc and calcium. It is best to buy organic where possible, as peaches have a thin skin and this can retain pesticides. Anyone allergic to other members of the Rosaceae family could be allergic to peaches (see Allergies & Intolerances on page 116).

Pears

The pear tree (Pyrus communis) belongs to the Rosaceae family. There are many different varieties of pears cultivated worldwide. Pears contain high amounts of fibre, especially in the skin, which supports the digestive system. They are rich in Vitamins C and K. Pears also contain small amounts of copper, potassium, manganese, magnesium, phosphorus, zinc, iron and calcium. It is best to buy organic and eat pears with their skin on. Anyone allergic to other members of the Rosaceae family could be allergic to pears (see Allergies & Intolerances on page 116).

Plums

There are many varieties and colours of plums (Prunus domestica) of which red is the most common. Plums are thought to support bone, gut, heart, and skin health, reduce inflammation and enhance immunity. They contain good amounts of fibre, potassium, copper, and Vitamins C, A and K. It is best to buy organic where possible. Anyone allergic to other members of the Rosaceae family could be allergic to plums (see Allergies & Intolerances on page 116).

Raspberries

Raspberries (Rubus idaeus) are bright red, black, purple or yellow berries, grown all over the world. They contain Vitamins C and K and the minerals manganese and calcium amongst others. Raspberries are thought to support bone, gut and heart health as well as enhance metabolism. It is best to buy organic, where possible, and wash just before use as raspberries can be contaminated with pesticides, bacteria or fungi. Anyone allergic to other members of the Rosaceae family could be allergic to raspberries (see Allergies & Intolerances on page 116).

Strawberries

Strawberries (Fragaria ananassa) are nutritionally dense, bright red berries covered in small seeds. They are a good source of Vitamin C, folate and manganese. Strawberries are thought to support brain, gut and heart health. It is best to buy organic strawberries where possible. Washing them in a mixture of water and vinegar may help to reduce contamination from bacteria and fungi. Those taking any medication, herbs or supplements to thin the blood should consult their physician before using strawberries therapeutically. Anyone allergic to other members of the Rosaceae family could be allergic to strawberries (see Allergies & Intolerances on page 116).

Sources

FARE Food Allergy Research and Education

www.foodallergy.org

This is a great website for learning about food allergies.

Linus Pauling Institute

www.lpi.oregonstate.edu

The Micronutrient Information Centre webpage gives access to information on macro and micronutrients, foods and dietary factors.

Natural Medicines

www.naturalmedicines.therapeuticresearch.com

This is a specialised subscription-based website that is useful for checking how food interacts with medications, supplements and herbs.

SELF Nutrition Data

www.nutritiondata.self.com

This website is helpful for information on the nutritional breakdown of our ingredients.

The World's Healthiest Foods by George Mateljan

www.whfoods.org

This book and website are useful as an overview of individual foods. They are an informative source of food related knowledge.

US Department of Agriculture

www.usda.gov

This website is useful for looking at the nutrient content of ingredients that are difficult to source elsewhere.

Suppliers & Resources

Supermarkets

Large supermarkets tend to stock most of the organic fruit, coconuts, oats, nuts, seeds and spices used in this book.

Local Indian and or Iranian/Middle Eastern stores generally have a good variety of nuts, seeds, spices and good quality saffron.

Whole Foods/Amazon.co.uk

Almost all the ingredients in this book can be found in the Whole Foods stores or on the Amazon website. The more uncommon ingredients such as hemp seeds and kelp can be found here.

www.buywholefoodsonline.co.uk

A family-run business based in Ramsgate, Kent. Has a great selection of organic nuts, seeds, kelp and cacao.

www.greensorganic.co.uk

Sells organic Hebridean kelp powder.

www.healthysupplies.co.uk

Great site for organic nuts and seeds. Great for buying in bulk.

www.thetigernutcompany.co.uk

Sells everything to do with tiger nuts, including the organic, whole (unpeeled) tiger nuts we use in our recipes. The tiger nuts are ethically sourced from Spain and Africa.

Kitchen Equipment

NutriBullet

All the milks in this book, except coconut, have been made in the NutriBullet. It is compact and does the job!

Vitamix

This is a bit more expensive and a whole lot bigger. It is super quick and especially useful for making coconut milk.

About the Authors

Dr Aparna Prinja is a trained physician and nutritionist in the UK. Her professional experiences made her realise that a balanced breakfast helps one attain better health. She is a proponent of the idea that plant-based milks have the power and untapped potential to kick-start the day.

Shital Shah is a UK-based caterer and former marketing analyst. An ardent food lover, since her childhood, she observed how her mother meticulously prepared fruits, vegetables and spices to transform the dietary habits of her diabetic father. Today, her private catering business focuses on the specific nutritional requirements of her clients and includes menus that are made without refined sugar, dairy or gluten.

Both Aparna and Shital grew up in Kenya and as children attended the Mombasa Academy. However, years later, the coincidence of their own children attending the same school in London established their friendship. On discovering a shared love of food and understanding how to maximise health benefits without compromising flavour, the pair combined their expertise to create a book of breakfast recipes. They quickly discovered that alternative milks alone could fill a whole book and Plant Milk Power, their first title, is the result. Influences sprung from the plants of their childhood, such as baobab, which is readily available in East Africa. Memories of the kitchens in their homes, the simple but therapeutic ingredients like turmeric (believed to be an all-purpose panacea) inspired their search for the right balance in the selection of ingredients. Aparna and Shital believe a resourceful kitchen can provide a cure for many common ailments, and they are excited to bring a fun approach to breakfast through their recipes for alternative milks, smoothies and chia bowls that are both nutritious and delicious!

Acknowledgements

Our sincere thanks to all those who helped in making this book possible:

Our loving husbands and families

The team at Meze Publishing

Xavier Buendia

Nandini Basuthakur

Dr Sumit Ghose

Dr Meera Shah

Rebecca Strong

Alpa Lakhani

Sangita Manek

Amy Sohanpaul

PLANT MILK
POWER

First edition printed in 2019 in the UK.

ISBN: 978-1-910863-41-1

Authors: Dr Aparna Prinja, Shital Shah

Preface: Nandini Basuthakur, Dr Sumit Ghose

About the Authors: Rebecca Strong

Edited by: Katie Fisher

Designed by: Paul Cocker

Photography by: Xavier Buendia

Additional photography by: Paul Cocker

Contributors: Sarah Koriba, David Wilson,
Izzy Randall, Amy Clarke, Sam Hancock,
Sally Zaki, Vanesa Balaj, Ruth Alexander,
Amelia Brownhill

me:ze
PUBLISHING

Published by Meze Publishing Limited
Unit 1b, 2 Kelham Square
Kelham Riverside
Sheffield S3 8SD
Web: www.mezepublishing.co.uk
Telephone: 0114 275 7709
Email: info@mezepublishing.co.uk